"A WESTERN ACROPOLIS OF LEARNING"
The University of California in 1897

Roy Lowe

Chapters in the History of the
University of California
Number Five

Center for Studies in Higher Education and
Institute of Governmental Studies
University of California, Berkeley
1996

Library of Congress Cataloging-In-Publication Data

Lowe, Roy.
  A western Acropolis of learning : the University of California in 1897 /
Roy Lowe.
     p. cm. -- (Chapters in the history of the University of California ; no.
5)
  Includes bibliographical references (p.).
  ISBN 0-87772-368-0
  1. University of California (1868-1952)--Buildings--History--19th century.
2. University of California, Berkeley--Buildings--History--19th century. I.
Title. II. Series.
LD759.L68 1996
378.794'67—dc20   96-33926
                                                  CIP

DEDICATION

for Sheldon Rothblatt

An unfailing friend to me and to my family. It is to his encourage-
ment, advice and unfailing support that the completion of this little
book is largely attributable.

In honor of the 125th anniversary of the founding of the University of California, the Center for Studies in Higher Education at Berkeley, in cooperation with the Institute of Governmental Studies, takes pleasure in publishing a series of "chapters" in the history of the University. These are designed to illuminate particular problems and periods in the history of U.C., especially its oldest and original campus at Berkeley, and to identify special turning points or features in the "long century" of the University's evolution. Histories are stories meant to be read and enjoyed in their own right, but the editors cannot conceal the hope that readers of these chapters will notice facts and ideas pertinent to the decade that closes our own century and millennium.

Carroll Brentano and
Sheldon Rothblatt, editors

Figure 1: Great Hall facade, University of Birmingham, Aston Webb, architect, 1900.

FOREWORD

Roy Lowe's title "A Western Acropolis of Learning" is taken from an appreciation of the events he describes at *The University of California in 1897* by a contemporary enthusiast for those events. As he tells us, the Phoebe Hearst International Competition for a new architectural plan for the University was an exciting event in northern California, and it put the University on the map, as it were, throughout the cultured world. It was the biggest and best-run public relations scheme in U.C.'s history.

Professor Lowe is British, and he enhances his California story with an insider's glimpse of the personalities involved in the struggle over the "vision," as we would call it today, proffered by the infant University of Birmingham (with which he was long associated) as it placed its idols on its facade. As an outsider at the Berkeley (and Palo Alto) scene, he offers a view of the people, the attitudes, and the allegiances here in the 1890s that may, today, discomfit the locals. He speaks of "racialized" attitudes and Immigration Restriction League memberships and often points out the particularly Anglo-Saxon sentiments of leading academics as well as Bay Area boosters. His avowed purpose is to "put into public discourse a view which is necessarily controversial" and inherently, to stage a sort of "battle of the styles," as he sees it, on the late nineteenth-century American campus.

To the local insider, Lowe's provocative story is something of a surprise. One had all along assumed that when Bernard Maybeck dismissed the cloisters of Oxbridge as being too cramped for huge numbers of students, and Olmsted complained about the idea of English lawns in California's desert climate, that Anglo-Saxonism, with its turn-of-the-century meaning of racial superiority, was hardly an element in the current decision making. But Lowe has challenged us, and perhaps this essay will arouse a new consideration of a possible more-than-local importance for the 1897 Competition.

Carroll Brentano

ACKNOWLEDGMENTS

Several people have helped both materially and practically in the preparation of this book. The staff of the University of California archive in the Bancroft Library have been unfailingly courteous and helpful over a series of visits as were the staff of the Stanford archive. Several British archivists are to be thanked, most notably Ben Benedikz, Christine Penney, and the staff of the Heslop Room at the University of Birmingham. My interest in the planning and design of colleges and universities in North America was first stimulated by a Visiting Fellowship at the Center for Studies in Higher Education at Berkeley more than a decade ago. The opportunity that the Center has given me for further visits has made it possible for me to pursue and develop this work to the point at which this book is now possible. Most recently a large debt of gratitude has been incurred to Valerie Guzman, who has painstakingly retyped and reworked the text, and also to Helen Joinson for helping to produce the final copy of the text. In particular, I owe a massive debt to Carroll Brentano for her detailed, careful, and always constructive comments on the manuscript, for her vital and enormous contribution to the selection, arrangement, and organization of the illustrations and for the enthusiasm and sense of fun that she has infused at every stage and that has maintained my appetite to complete the work at five thousand miles distance. This is a subject on which she is authoritative, and she has generously shared that expertise with me in a spirit of true scholarship.

ILLUSTRATIONS

Figure 2: Memorial Arch, Stanford University, Charles A. Coolidge, architect, circa 1905, illustrating the California heritage.

"A WESTERN ACROPOLIS OF LEARNING"
THE UNIVERSITY OF CALIFORNIA IN 1897

Roy Lowe

No one who has considered the differences in social,
moral, and intellectual outlook between the Californian and
the inhabitant either of the Middle West or of the eastern
states, can doubt that California will develop in the course
of time a society and a civilization differing in certain
essential respects from that of the rest of the country . . . it
is possible that the most characteristic expression of
California's peculiar phase of Americanism will be found
in the intellectual sphere. . . . This prophecy exists in the
minds of the enlightened Californians as a living
aspiration.[1]

The Berkeley campus offers an enduring testament to a
particular moment in history. It is at once peculiarly Californian
and yet European. Symbolically, even iconographically, the
Berkeley Acropolis is the outcome of a national effort by Americans to capture the best of European architectural styles and city
planning while somehow conveying a sense of the special qualities
of the New World. At times, the task seemed forced, extravagantly
conceived and self absorbed, but for the historian of universities the
story wonderfully illuminates the dilemmas and the successes of the
modern university.

The search for a suitable style and plan for a university in
California is of particular interest because it was part of a more
widespread late-nineteenth century Anglo-American quest for an
appropriate identity. At a time when there were many new
foundations, as well as significant expansion of the existing
European universities, the first impulse was to turn to the great
models for university construction: in England that meant neoclas-

---

[1]Herbert Croly, "The New University of California," *Architectural
Record* (April 1908): 2, 6.

sical and neogothic. Only in the second half of the nineteenth century did the leading English university architects, such as T. G. Jackson and Alfred Waterhouse, begin to use Renaissance styles. Jackson began the fashion with the Examination Halls at Oxford: within a few years Waterhouse had produced his extravagant designs for Keble College at the same university. In no time at all Basil Champneys, the well-known civic and domestic architect was employing the currently fashionable Queen Anne style at Newnham College, Cambridge. Their work, and that of several copyists at the ancient universities in England, raised the question of whether, if a university wished to be distinctive, it should choose one of the neohistorical styles in use at the time, or did other possibilities exist? This problem plagued the planners of the new universities in England as well as those American architects charged with the expansion of higher education across the breadth of the United States. So, to approach an analysis of the influences at work at Berkeley, this chapter will begin with an English example before moving on to look at the broader context of American university planning.

THE ENGLISH CONTEXT

In the spring of 1899 Joe Chamberlain, sometime mayor of Birmingham and now a key figure at Westminster, wrote to Andrew Carnegie to ask for financial support for the University College at Birmingham, which Chamberlain was keen to develop. Carnegie, a Scot who had made a fortune in Pittsburgh in the steel industry, offered 50,000 pounds to what he called "the Pittsburgh of the old land," explaining that those involved in the American steel industry had a debt of honor to the land of Bessemer, of Siemens, and of Thomas. The correspondence between the two men shows that during the few months that followed they had their wires badly crossed. Chamberlain intended to spend the money on the best teachers money could buy: Carnegie refused to go ahead with the gift unless it was spent on buildings. Chamberlain argued that the existing buildings in the city center would suffice. Carnegie was so outraged at this philistinism that he sent expenses for three members of staff at Birmingham to visit North America, insisting

Figure 3: Aston Webb buildings, University of Birmingham, 1900.

that they have a look at Cornell, Stevens, Ann Arbor, and Yale.[2] They took in McGill at Montreal too, and returned full of what they had seen. Their report opened Chamberlain's eyes, and he become the strongest advocate of a new campus away from the center of the city. It was Chamberlain who looked to Aston Webb, one of the best known Victorian architects, to design the buildings, and Chamberlain who, after a visit to Siena in 1904, insisted on lavish expenditure on a campanile that still dominates the campus much as does the Sather Tower at Berkeley (Figure 3).

The parallels between Birmingham and Berkeley are clear and tell us much about what informed university planners on both sides of the Atlantic at the turn of the century. First, there was a growing awareness of the importance of the physical environment of colleges and schools. Second, there was a perceived need to discover what was going on elsewhere and to ensure that new undertakings were comprehensible within an established convention of academic planning. Third, as Carnegie's aside makes clear, what impelled these college builders was a world view, which in retrospect we may see as racialized, and that certainly involved elements of what Stuart Anderson and other commentators have called "Anglo-Saxonism." The attempt here is to try to show how this came to be worked out at Berkeley, but before we leave the shores of Albion, it is pertinent to say a little more about the details of the Birmingham buildings, because the questions that arose around their design can also tell us something about what was in the minds of the Berkeley designers.

Chamberlain and Carnegie were clear, and were agreed that what they wanted was a school of science, linking with the local industries of the West Midlands of England. As Carnegie put it, in one of his letters to Chamberlain: "If I were in your place I should recognize the futility of trying to rival Oxford and Cambridge. . . . Birmingham should make the scientific the principal department,

---

[2]Carnegie to Chamberlain, June 3, 1899, University of Birmingham archival collection, 1960/I/3/1-2.

the Classical subsidiary . . . taking our Cornell University as its model."[3]

Accordingly, Aston Webb, a leading English architect of the day, was instructed to find an architectural style that would reflect this commitment to science. He was, of course, well aware that at both Oxford and Cambridge the major expansion of the colleges during the previous 30 years had been accomplished through the use of beautiful Renaissance styles of architecture, which architects like T. G. Jackson were using to confirm a commitment to a humane education. Clearly, something different was needed at Birmingham. In a situation in which science and technology, or applied science, were to be the university's main *raison d'être*, Palladian architecture, because it was considered itself to be a scientific style and suggested scientific ideas like proportion and symmetry, might have been thought appropriate. Yet, by the mid-nineteenth century, it was no longer clear that "Palladian," as a style, carried these precise connotations. The need was for a style that would suggest new science: at the lowest level, it had to be different. The solution that Webb came up with was remarkably similar to that devised in the same year by Ralph Adams Cram, the American architect for the Rice Institute at Houston, Texas. Byzantine was the style both plumped for in a college of applied science. (Figure 1) Webb, returning to his London office after showing his first drawings to the Birmingham building committee told his apprentices exultantly, "They've swallowed the lot!"[4] We have from Cram a more considered account of why this style was appropriate, and I quote from it now because it is an explanation that neatly and unwittingly links Birmingham to Berkeley.

A college was to be created *de novo* in Texas. What to do? Here was a plain-like area with no cultural traditions except those of the flimsiest with Mexico. Racially it was New England, culturally it was Middle West. What style

---

[3]Carnegie to Chamberlain, May 9, 1899, Birmingham archival collection, 1960/I/3/1-2.

[4]H. B. Cresswell, "Sir Aston Webb and his Office," in *Edwardian Architecture and its Origins* (London, 1975), ed. Alastair Service, 331.

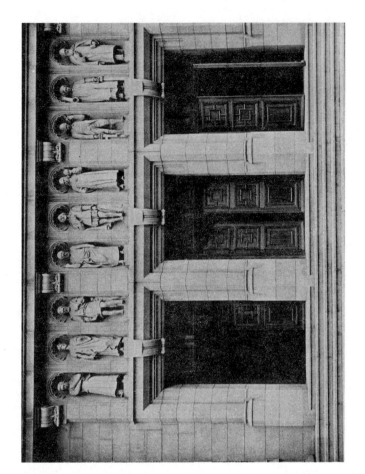

Figure 4: Detail of the portico of the Great Hall, University of Birmingham, showing the final outcome of the debate on whom should be represented.

could be used . . . ? Renaissance of Mexico? Colonial of
New England? Collegiate   Gothic? None seemed really
possible under the circumstances. . . . No! This college had
to suggest the learning and culture that reached back,
essentially unchanged, through Oxford, Paris, Heidelberg,
to Salerno, Cordoba, Byzantium and so to Alexandria,
Athens, Thebes and Memphis. For this reason a quite new
theory was postulated, thus: Mediaeval art was the result
very largely of religious fervour under monasticism
working itself out through the fresh and uncorrupted blood
of Northern races. . . . Now suppose that this great religious
revival . . . had operated, not on the rude, though lusty
barbarians from the North, but on the Latin races of Italy,
Spain and France? What would have been the result? The
first buildings at Houston are an attempted answer.[5]

So, it seems that at least one college planner may have been alert to
the possibilities of playing northern and southern Europe against
each other in the buildings, using the style to locate new institutions
within their communities and to say something about the nature of
those communities in the process.

Equally, it was important to make some reference to the
northern European Renaissance if the college was to be seen as fully
committed to the highest principles of academic life. At Birmingham, Joseph Chamberlain's speeches showed a growing concern
during the early years to make sure that "general culture" was being
taught as well as the applied sciences. The amusing fight over
exactly who should be depicted in the nine niches over the main
doorway of the great hall tells us something about the tension
between Arts and Sciences. (Figure 4) The final line-up had
Newton, Shakespeare, and Plato in the middle, Michelangelo,
Virgil, and Beethoven to the left (Beethoven preferred over Bach
because he had "an impressive figure for sculpture"), and to the
right, Darwin, Faraday, and Watt: a fair working compromise
between Arts and Sciences, local and universal, but arrived at only

---

[5]Ralph Adams Cram, "Have I a Philosophy of Design?" *Pencil Points*
(November 13, 1932): 730.

after the infant Commerce Faculty had put in a strong bid for Adam Smith. Archimedes nearly got in but was dismissed as "too shadowy," one member of staff proposed Emmanuel Kant as "the greatest mediaeval philosopher," a judgment that didn't promise much from the new philosophy department. Priestley was left out as "not comfortable in such company," and the first professor of physics, with a startling lack of imagination, wanted Edward VI in the middle, with Edward VII and Josiah Mason on either side of him.[6]

This may smack of antiquarian detail, but it is a detail that tells us much about the anxiety of these founding fathers to be sure that their new university struck the right resonances in its buildings. They were part of, and alert to, a set of historic associations that any university planner in the English speaking world could ignore at his or her peril at the turn of the twentieth century.

THE ANGLO-SAXON CONTEXT

What makes all this meaningful for Berkeley is the overwhelming power of Anglo-Americanism within academic life during the late nineteenth century. This made it virtually inevitable that any discussion of the best campus design for a Californian university would take place in the shadow of Oxbridge. Anglo-Americanism was a vital element in the planning of universities precisely because it was most fully articulated by a group of academics who subscribed to the view that universities were the most potent force for preserving all that was best in modern civilization in a quickly changing world,[7] and the changes that particularly caught their attention were new patterns of immigration into the United States. It was in this vein that Carnegie, in his negotiations with Chamberlain, had added an explanatory note to his offer of funding for Birmingham, stressing that "You know I have at heart the coopera-

---

[6]Eric William Ives, *Image of a University: The Great Hall at Edgbaston, 1900-1909*, inaugural lecture, University of Birmingham (Birmingham, 1988).

[7]Stuart Anderson, *Race and Rapprochement* (London, 1981), 14-59.

tion of our English speaking race, but I wish to save our half [presumably Britain, as both men were British by birth] from subject races and foreign warfare."[8]

In England, such leading historians as Maitland, Kemble, Froude, Stubbs, J. R. Green, and E. A. Freeman ("the prince of Teutonists") were all subscribers to the creed of Anglo-Saxonism at the same time that George Bancroft was dispensing his personal vision of Romantic Nationalism in the United States. Freeman toured the eastern seaboard in 1881 and 1882, telling his enrapt audiences that they were "the inheritors of the freedom for which Godwine strove in one age and Hampden in another: I claim you as brethren."[9] Freeman found a particularly receptive ear in Herbert Baxter Adams, who entertained him at Johns Hopkins and two years later founded the American Historical Society. Adams taught Woodrow Wilson, who himself became a university teacher.

Stuart Anderson has shown the strength of this Anglo-Saxonism on both sides of the Atlantic, based on a

> belief that the civilization of the English speaking nations was superior to that of any other people on the planet . . . that the primacy of the English and American civilization was largely due to the innate racial superiority of the people who were descended from the Anglo-Saxon invaders of Britain.[10]

In this vein, the Reverend Washington Gladden told an English audience in 1898 that "the constructive ideas of our civilization are Anglo-Saxon ideas."[11] It was a Berkeley alumnus, Frank Norris, who, in his most famous work, *The Octopus*, sharply contrasted the simplicity, honesty, directness, beauty and strength of the Anglo-Saxon farmers of the San Joaquin Valley with the degenerate

---

[8]Andrew Carnegie to Joseph Chamberlain, March 30, 1899, University of Birmingham archival collection, 1960/I/3/1-2.

[9]E. A. Freeman, *Lectures to American Audiences* (Philadelphia, 1882), 55. Godwine and Hampden were both seen by Victorians as defenders of individual liberty in England.

[10]Anderson, *Race*, 12.

[11]*Ibid.*

attitudes and appearance of their Portuguese and Mexican employees.[12]

But, if any one university can be identified as the seedbed of this Anglo-Saxonism, it was surely Harvard, where James Russell Lowell exercised an enduring influence on Henry Adams and John Fiske, who shared lodgings as students. Fiske made four lecture tours to England and included a talk on "Manifest Destiny" among his baggage. Other Harvard Anglophiles were Albert Bushnell Hart, John Lothrop Motley, Francis Parkman, Brooks Adams, and, among the alumni, two of the best known Anglo-Saxonists, Theodore Roosevelt and Henry Cabot Lodge. Leon C. Marshall, the economist, was a student at Harvard and began his teaching career there. He became a committee member of the organization that might best be described as the "political wing" of this Anglo-Saxon movement, the Immigration Restriction League. Francis A. Walker, president of the Massachusetts Institute of Technology, who, as we shall see, was frequently turned to for advice on campus planning, was a vice president of the Immigration Restriction League (IRL) and on one occasion referred to new immigrants to the United States as "beaten men from beaten races; representing the worst failures in the struggle for existence."[13] It was to Walker that Leland Stanford was to turn in 1886. Another leading figure in the Immigration Restriction League was A. Lawrence Lowell, president of Harvard. Lowell was a close personal friend of the architect C. A. Coolidge, who became involved in the planning of over a dozen American colleges.

Another committee member of the IRL was David Starr Jordan, whom Leland Stanford chose as first president of his university. Jordan was on record as saying that "only the Saxon and the Goth know the meaning of freedom . . . it is well for us to remember that we came of hardy stock. The Anglo-Saxon race, with its strengths and virtues, was born of hard times."[14] In respect to immigration,

---

[12]Anderson, *Race*, 59.

[13]*Ibid.*

[14]Kevin Starr, *Americans and the California Dream* (Oxford, 1973), 309.

this meant that Jordan was fully in accord with the IRL line and was one of its strongest advocates. "At Castle Garden in New York we should turn back . . . those whose descendents are likely through incompetence and vice to be a permanent burden on our social or political order."[15]

The existence of this intellectual network leads me to ask how far the new American campuses of the turn of the century can be seen as artifacts of this ideology of Anglo-Saxonism. We can certainly find echoes of these ideas in the debate on the Berkeley campus. In 1898, for example, a San Francisco newspaper reported the response of Norman Shaw, a leading English architect, to the announcement of the result of the design competition for the University of California. Shaw was upset that the competition had been such a triumph for Beaux Arts architects, commenting ruefully that he could not help feeling

> a regret that a university for the English speaking race should not be modelled on English designs. The university towns of Oxford and Cambridge, St. Paul's and the finest structures of Inigo Jones might all suggest models for a university in thorough keeping with the genius of the Anglo-Saxon race.[16]

THE CALIFORNIA CONTEXT

If one important element in the debate on the Berkeley campus was this network of ideas that was international in scope, another was the northern Californian context, which gave an urgency to the quest for a city of learning that could win international acclaim. During the late-1880s and 1890s contracts for important buildings in and around San Francisco went increasingly to architects of national and even international repute, as what had already become the seventh largest city in the United States sought to escape its

---

[15]Starr, *Americans*, 310.

[16]*San Francisco Examiner*, 1898. See University of California, Berkeley, Bancroft Library, Hearst Competition press notices, (308 gh pr. vi).

Figure 5: Bernard Maybeck

reputation for lawlessness and licentiousness. One of the clearest tokens of this transition was the appearance in San Francisco in 1888 of an architect whose reputation was already established on the East Coast, Arthur Page Brown, invited to design a mausoleum for the recently deceased president of the Southern Pacific Railroad. In the following year, 1889, Brown decided to move his offices to San Francisco permanently in an attempt, as one historian has put it, to devise

a new American art and architecture, inspired by an assimi-
lation to American purposes of the best of the European
past, an academic eclecticism that would repossess and
reenergize the high forms of the Classical and Renaissance
past with new American energy.[17]

Brown had the perfect credentials for this role: trained with McKim, Mead and White, an eminent architectural firm, much of whose work was in the Renaissance style, in New York, he had traveled in Europe for two years, familiarizing himself with the best French, Italian, and English architecture at first hand and setting up an informal attachment to the Paris École des Beaux Arts. Brown recruited to San Francisco A. C. Schweinfurth, and among the galaxy of young talent he attracted to work with him were Willis Polk and Bernard Maybeck, who was later to become a key figure at Berkeley. (Figure 5) Although Brown was to die young in 1896, he was possibly the most significant among those who were anxious to establish a San Francisco style at the end of the nineteenth century, and in his work on the Crocker building and the Ferry Building, as well as the numerous commissions he took for private residences, it became clear that this distinctive architecture was to be one that was drawn from European models. It was clear, too, both from his writing and contemporary debate, that this style should extend beyond domestic and private architecture to great civic undertakings. Brown himself wanted a great civic center modeled on the Ringstrasse in Vienna, and it was in this spirit that

---

[17]Kevin Starr, *Inventing the Dream* (Oxford, 1985), 176-98; and Starr, *Americans*, 365-414.

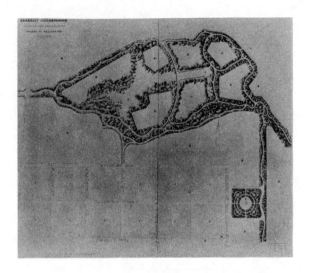

Figure 6: Frederick Law Olmsted's plan for the College of California, 1866.

Phoebe Hearst turned her attention to the planning of the University of California.

The urgency of this task was highlighted by another development that threatened to overshadow the state university, and this was the establishment of a private university by Leland Stanford at Palo Alto. It was at Palo Alto that the themes of the civilizing of California and the creation of a city of learning came together, although perhaps not for the first time.

Stanford was bent on the creation of an architecture that he called "distinctly Californian in character,"[18] a theme taken up by the *Sacramento Record Union,* which was only one of the several local newspapers anticipating a university at Palo Alto that would break away from the model of Oxford and Cambridge and would be, as the editor put it, peculiarly Californian.[19] Nonetheless, Leland Stanford was well aware of the need to consult in the east before embarking on his project. He visited Yale, Harvard, Cornell, and MIT to gather ideas, and consulted in particular Francis A. Walker, president of MIT, and A. D. White of Cornell. Both of these men were familiar with the work of Frederick Law Olmsted, who was and remains best known for his planning of public parks, but who was already influential in the field of campus planning.

Olmsted had drawn the first campus plan for Berkeley between 1864 and 1866, (Figure 6) and one fragment of his correspondence that survives from that time makes clear what he had been trying to achieve there. He insisted that "the erection of buildings will be no interruption to the view," and hoped that those moving around the Berkeley campus would be treated to "occasional distant views and complete landscapes." He confessed himself "reluctant to recommend greensward." Olmsted's commitment to a very English ideal of a controlled landscape set in parkland was confirmed when he described the way in which:

---

[18]Starr, *Americans,* 316.
[19]*Sacramento Record Union* (July 3, 1886); see also Paul Venable Turner, Marcia E. Vetrocq, and Karen Weitze, *The Founders and the Architects: The Design of Stanford University* (Stanford, 1976), 58.

in the large Eastern colleges the original design, of arrang-
ing all the buildings . . . in a symmetrical way has in every
case been found impracticable and has been given up,
which so far as it has been carried out is a cause of great
perplexity to those at present concerned.[20]

Although he was surprised at the way in which symmetrical site
planning had been abandoned elsewhere in the United States, he
was certainly not insisting on any such arrangement at Berkeley.
He thought the development of what one historian has called a
"naturalistic park"[21] would give the best chance of integrating
domestic life, suburban requirements, and academic considerations.
For many nineteenth- century Americans the wilderness was seen
as America's park: here Olmsted had been seeking to tame that
wilderness within a European idiom.

Richard P. Dober, an historian of American campus development, has commented that, when Olmsted first visited Berkeley, it
was unoccupied territory,[22] although the grid of roads on the south
side of campus was already planned. Olmsted emphasized that "the
first requirement of a plan for Berkeley's improvement is that it
should present sufficient inducements to the formation of refined
and elegant homes in the immediate vicinity of the proposed college
buildings."[23] This was also in the minds of many English planners
of schools and colleges: at Eastbourne, Bedford, and Cheltenham,
as well as other towns, new schools were set out in a grid of roads
with a view to attracting middle-class residents to the district.

By the 1880s Olmsted was an old hand, having been involved
in campus planning at the University of Massachusetts at Amherst,
Cornell, the land grant college at Orono in Maine, and directly
influencing many others. He was, therefore, a likely candidate to
become Stanford's key adviser on his grounds at Palo Alto. What

---

[20]Bancroft Library, University Archives, Regents' records, CU 1, 20:2.

[21]Loren W. Partridge, *John Galen Howard and the Berkeley Campus*
(Berkeley, 1978), 8.

[22]Richard P. Dober, *Campus Planning* (New York, 1963), 34.

[23]Olmsted to Stanford, November 27, 1886, Stanford University
archives, Stanford collection, 1,1.

developed between the two men was a running battle on how exactly to interpret in practice the perceived need for an identifiably Californian seat of learning. In November 1886 Olmsted warned Stanford in a long and detailed letter, of the need to guard against the attractions of a predominantly English model. He emphasized the ways in which the English in India,

after an experience there of nearly two centuries, still order their lives in various particulars with absurd disregard of requirements of comfort and health imposed by the climate, because they cannot dismiss from their minds standards of style, propriety and taste which are the result of their fathers' training under different climactic conditions.[24]

This is a lesson which must not be overlooked in planning this new seat of learning:

I have been led more and more to feel that a permanently suitable plan for a great university in California must be studied with constant watchfulness against certain tendencies from which neither you, nor General Walker [president of MIT] . . . can reasonably be supposed to be free.

He went on to suggest that the principles which were being followed in campus planning, both in England, at Oxford and Cambridge, and in the Ivy League institutions were to be avoided:

[f]or a great university in California, ideals must be given up that . . . we have been led to regard as appropriate in the outward aspect of Eastern and English colleges. If we are to look for types of buildings and arrangements suitable to the climate of California, it will rather be in these founded by the wiser men of Syria, Greece, Italy and Spain. . . . You will remember in what a different way from the English methods . . . the open spaces about nearly all buildings you have seen in the south of Europe to which throngs of people resort, have been treated. In the great "front yard" of St. Peter's . . . not a tree, nor a bush, nor a particle of turf, has been made use of.[25]

---

[24] *Ibid.*
[25] *Ibid.*

Olmsted added gloomily that the buildings already erected at Berkeley (i.e., North and South Halls) were a warning of how mistaken it was to assume that what made for beauty and comfort on the eastern seaboard would work in the Californian climate, in which they quickly became "unsuitable, dreary and forlorn." He predicted that sooner or later all the existing Berkeley buildings would have to come down, in just the same way that demolition work had recently been done at Amherst.

> What I have in mind at Berkeley is not alone that the buildings are in a cheap and nasty style, but that the disposition of them and of all the grounds and offices about them betrays heedlessness of the requirements of convenience and comfort under the conditions of the situation and climate.[26] (Frontispiece)

It was at about the same time that Olmsted complained privately that Leland Stanford

> seemed to be bent on giving his university New England scenery, New England trees and turf . . . nobody thinks of anything in gardening that will not be thoroughly unnatural to it.[27]

Once Stanford had absorbed these ideas, his architect was instructed to turn to southern Europe for inspiration. (Figure 7) The architect in question was C. A. Coolidge, who had traveled across America to present himself to Governor Stanford in order to win the contract. Coolidge, together with Shepley and Rutan, had inherited the office of H. H. Richardson, one of the founding fathers of American romanesque architecture, so this call for something in the southern European tradition was one they were well qualified to meet.

What followed was to be of significance for Berkeley. As the planning of Stanford University went ahead, the power battle between Olmsted and Stanford was one that Governor Stanford was bound to win. The result was a series of changing demands, as

---

[26]*Ibid.*

[27]Olmsted to Charles Eliot, July 20, 1886. Stanford University archives, Stanford collection, box 2.

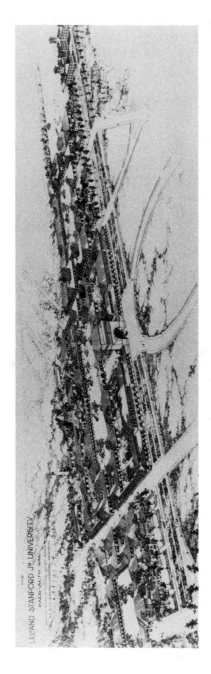

Figure 7: Design for Stanford University, Shepley, Rutan and Coolidge, architects, circa 1888.

Stanford sought first to accommodate and later to control Olmsted's ideas. In the face of these revised ideas, Coolidge fell back on the designs that had been left in the files of the now deceased Richardson. The Memorial Arch at Stanford became an almost exact copy of an unexecuted Civil War memorial for Buffalo, except that the subject of the frieze was Californian rather than national. (Figure 8) Coolidge was an admirer of the twelfth century cathedral at Salamanca and throughout his career kept to hand the drawings he had made of it on a youthful tour. Now they came out to make the model for the tower of the new Memorial Church at Palo Alto in response to the governor's reinterpretation of the advice he was getting from Olmsted that southern European models were the most appropriate. But the church itself was copied from Richardson's original drawings for the Trinity Church at Boston with a tower stolen from Spain.[28]

It was a model of how, in practice, not to proceed with the building of a university campus, and, as such, it must surely have left messages for those Californians involved only a few years later in the planning of a state university. It also left an unfinished agenda. From the start, Stanford had talked about a town growing up around the university and of the need to build grade schools and other facilities for the community that would appear. All this had to be abandoned on grounds of cost. Central to Stanford's modifications of the original Olmsted-Coolidge plans was the demand for axiality that would allow for orderly later expansion of the site. This too worked to determine the agenda of future Californian planners. Indeed, while all this was going on, John Galen Howard, in the employ of Shepley, Rutan and Coolidge, was working on the Stanford drawings for Coolidge—Howard was to become the architect of the University of California: the link with Berkeley could hardly have been more direct!

Despite the delays, by the end of 1887, *The San Francisco Newsletter* was making great play of the ways in which the new buildings at Stanford were helping to shape the identity of California itself. The frieze for the new memorial arch, one of the center

---

[28]Turner, et al., *The Founders*, 40-43.

Figure 8: Inner quad and Memorial Arch, Stanford University, circa 1905.

pieces of the Stanford campus, was self-consciously southern European, but at the same time celebrated:

> the progress of California, starting with the aboriginal Indian . . . a series of reliefs depicting the history of the State, in its Indian, its Spanish and its American eras. In the latter will be subdivisions celebrating the gold fever, the agricultural development, the railroad competition, and, as a natural culmination, the founding of the university.[29]

(Figure 2)

THE AMERICAN CONTEXT

If, by the end of the 1880s, universities were coming to be seen in California as one of the highest embodiment in bricks and mortar of the ideals of the state, it has to be said that their construction took place within the context of a broad tradition of town and campus planning already well-established in North America and heavily derivative from Europe. It was Thomas Jefferson, two centuries before, who gave to Pierre Charles L'Enfant, a French engineer, maps of European cities to assist his planning of a new capital city for the United States. Benjamin Latrobe, William Thornton, Charles Bullfinch and the Irishman James Hogan were among the European pioneers of planning in North America. By the late-nineteenth century, town and campus planning was well-established in the United States, and Californians were simply confirming their commitment to the Union by seeking so ardently to work within this tradition. It is worth reminding ourselves, too, that Leland Stanford lived throughout his childhood only two miles from J. J. Ramée's Union College at Schenechtady in New York State. It is perhaps, then, hardly surprising that as a Californian, at a later point in his life he should seek to build a university within this broad American planning tradition.

---

[29]*San Francisco Newsletter*, December 25, 1888.

Indeed, by the late-nineteenth century there had grown up an American tradition of collegiate design.[30] Perhaps the best-known early model is Thomas Jefferson's plan of an "academical village" for the University of Virginia drawn up in the years following 1817. But Ramée's drawings for Union College, dating from 1813, have been called "the first realized campus plan in the United States" and were followed by many more campus designs as the century wore on. Over 500 new colleges were planned before the Civil War, and public support for state universities after 1865 helped to contribute to a tripling of enrollments during the final third of the century. With this growth came a series of experiments in campus design, perhaps most notably the Towne and Davis plan for Ann Arbor (1838), Trinity College, Hartford, Connecticut, designed by William Burges in 1878, and John Stewardson's 1895 designs for the University of Pennsylvania. In one important sense, the development of the Berkeley campus was no more and no less than another increment in a developing American tradition. It is to the precise circumstances of that development, which were to make it in both appearance and reality a key moment in the history of American universities, that we will now turn.

THE BERKELEY COMPETITION

The College of California, predecessor of the University, was originally set up in Oakland in 1855, the location reflecting the fact that the trustees feared the corrupting influence of an urban site: they sought "to give the college for all time the benefits of a country location."[31] Within three years Horace Bushnell had sought but others had found what was to be the permanent home of the University, on the Berkeley site, although the name was only acquired later. It was favored as being conveniently situated with

---

[30]Paul Venable Turner, *Campus: An American Planning Tradition* (Cambridge, Mass., 1984) is, for the present, the basis for any discussion of campus planning in the United States.

[31]Partridge, *Howard*, 6.

respect to San Francisco, being in full view of the city, and yet sufficiently removed to be beyond objectionable proximity.[32]

Olmsted's first campus plan, as we have already seen, was intended to emphasize this rusticity by promoting an irregular park plan, although he did incorporate a short central allée—which remained in all later designs. (Figure 6) Olmsted emphasized that he would

> contemplate the erection of no buildings for college purposes . . . except as detached structures, each designed by itself. . . . In other words I would propose to adopt a picturesque rather than a formal and perfectly symmetrical arrangement, for the two reasons that the former would better harmonize artistically with the general character desired for the neighborhood, and that it would allow any enlargement or modification of the general plan.[33]

This reflected a nationwide interest in parks, itself a reaction to urbanization whose worst excesses were nowhere more evident than in San Francisco.

When, in 1868, the College was incorporated into the University of California, Olmsted's plan was supplanted by a new design executed by David Farquharson and Henry Kenitzer. This involved a sweeping arc of buildings in French Second Empire (Mansard) style, with a curving approach avenue. This was a fashionable style at that time, and in adopting it the University of California was following the example of Vassar College, and of Mills College in Oakland, designed by Samuel Bugbee. South Hall, which survives, was built to this plan, and its erection was personally supervised by Farquharson.[34]

Several developments led to the 1890s becoming the decade when it was seen to be imperative to move beyond this. We have already seen the pressures that were growing for the establishment of a new image for northern California. One of the students at

---

[32] William Ferrier, *Origins and Development of the University of California* (Berkeley, 1930), 163.

[33] Partridge, *Howard*, 7.

[34] *Ibid.*, 7-9.

Berkeley reflected ruefully in 1892 that "none of the buildings here compare in beauty with the Leland Stanford University,"[35] and in November 1890 a petition supported by 265 students was presented to the Grounds and Buildings Committee asking for swift action "to improve the students' campus and vicinity, in such a manner as to render it fit and suitable for athletic contests of all kinds."[36] A sudden upturn in enrollments during the early 1890s made the question of new buildings imperative: one increasingly important figure was Frank Soulé, professor of civil engineering. It was Soulé who, at the start of 1891, organized a thorough inspection and survey of the "campus" (i.e., the athletic grounds used by students) and found it to be "in a state of nature . . . and a little too small for the field games usually played in this university."[37] A month later, as a precondition of more extensive improvements, Soule proposed, and then conducted, the first properly surveyed map of the whole campus ("a complete map of the university domain").[38]

By February 1892, the Grounds and Buildings Committee was beginning to plan for "certain highly important improvements on the university grounds." The Committee reported to the Regents that it had

> been in consultation with a distinguished professional landscape engineer who was architect of the Jackson Park of Chicago and of the St. Louis Park at St. Louis, Missouri, but before much progress had been made, his death suddenly intervened and nothing was accomplished. These matters being urgent, new plans of the grounds should be formulated for their development and ornamentation and for the designation and reservation of building sites.[39]

The landscape engineer in question was almost certainly John Wellborn Root, who was consulting engineer for the refurbishment

[35]*Ibid.* 9.
[36]Bancroft Library, University Archives, CU 1, 20:2. Petition signed by 265 students to the Grounds Committee.
[37]University Archives, CU 1, 20:3.
[38]*Ibid.*
[39]*Ibid.*

of Jackson Park in Chicago to accommodate the 1893 Columbian Exposition, but who died suddenly of pneumonia during 1891. It is a connection that puts the Berkeley planners in direct touch with the Chicago World's Fair, where French influences were paramount. It was a chance conversation between Frank Soulé and Bernard Maybeck that led to Maybeck leaving Brown's architectural office in San Francisco to begin teaching at Berkeley. When Maybeck took up his post he found a developing furor over the layout of the Berkeley campus. Jacob Reinstein, an attorney and alumnus recently appointed to the regents, had suggested that the university erect a main entrance at the west end of the site towards the Golden Gate. However, the Building Committee, chaired by J. West Martin, was loath to approve a development that threatened "the most beautiful and attractive portion of the university domain, covered with a grove of magnificent oaks, ranked among the most beautiful in the world."

This minute went on to show clearly the growing determination to commit to root and branch refurbishment of the Berkeley campus:

> Your committee have deemed it best . . . to recommend the selection and appointment of a suitable person to prepare such permanent and general plans of the university site as will meet with the approbation of your honourable body, that all reorganization of present plans be held in abeyance until definite plans are adopted, also: that an Architect of experience and ability be selected to consider the whole subject architecturally with reference to the location of all buildings on the university grounds, so that the present buildings and the buildings to be erected hereafter may be grouped together in a harmonious whole.[40]

Once in post, Bernard Maybeck soon began to lobby for an extension to the University of the building boom that was overtaking the Bay Area, and, as a graduate of the École des Beaux Arts, he had no doubts from the outset about the direction that it should take. It was Maybeck who, in 1894, proposed to Reinstein the idea

---

[40]University Archives, CU 1, 20:4.

of an architectural competition for the Berkeley campus. Reinstein had only recently been appointed to the University regents and quickly became an enthusiast for the idea. It became a financial possibility when the interest of the heiress Phoebe Hearst was engaged. (Figure 9)

By October 1896, she was in correspondence with Reinstein, setting in motion what was to become one of the most remarkable architectural events of the late- nineteenth century. She wrote:

> I am deeply impressed with the proposition now before the Board of Regents to determine upon a comprehensive and permanent plan for the buildings and grounds of the University of California. . . . I should be glad to aid in its complete and speedy realisation I am more anxious for this, as I have in contemplation the erection on the university grounds of the two buildings, one of them to be the memorial referred to [one the Hearst School of Mining and the other the womens' Gymnasium which female students have petitioned for]. I would therefore suggest that I be permitted to contribute the funds necessary to obtain, by international competition, plans for the fitting architectural improvement of the university grounds at Berkeley. . . . I have only one wish in this matter—that the plans adopted should be worthy of the great university whose material home they are to provide for . . . and that they should redound to the glory of the state whose culture and civilization are to be nursed and developed at the university.[41]

It was in this same letter that she suggested the release of Bernard Maybeck "who has been identified with the idea of this plan from its inception" for two years of travel in the eastern states and in Europe "to facilitate a proper understanding of our design among architects."[42] Reinstein's official response anticipated

> buildings which shall body forth the power and the dignity of a sovereign State . . . making patriotism and a lofty re-

---

[41]University Archives, CU 1, 20:11.
[42]*Ibid.*

Figure 9: Phoebe Apperson Hearst, as frontispiece of *The International Competition for the Phoebe Hearst Architectural Plan for the University of California*, 1899.

gard for the State as certain a result of a course at this University as a love for what is beautiful and true.[43]

This determination to devise an architectural scheme worthy of the new educational republic that was to be created coincided with the rise of the City Beautiful movement, for which the 1893 Columbia Exposition in Chicago had been seminal. As we have already seen, the Berkeley planners consulted at least one of the Chicago landscape engineers. The Worlds Fair gave leading architects, among them Hunt, McKim, and Sullivan, the chance to arrange a series of white palaces around a formal court. It was here, too, that Emile Bénard was thought to have staked his claim for a place in the first rank of internationally recognized architects. As winner of the 1867 Prix de Rome and a rising star in the Beaux Arts firmament, he was credited with the contract for the arts building of the Chicago Exposition that became "the most admired of the many buildings on the ground."[44] The exposition offered "a vision of what public buildings and their surroundings might be,"[45] and marked the moment of acceptance in North America for Beaux Arts styles. The implications for collegiate design were quickly realized:

> Just as the Exposition gave incentive to the City Beautiful movement, with its imposition of boulevards and monumental axes of differentiated architecture, so too did new designers of new colleges and old find in its principles of arranging spaces and buildings a method for giving some control to campus growth.[46]

Accordingly, when the Berkeley competition was announced, with rules translated into four languages to ensure a genuinely international contest, the sponsors emphasized that what they wanted was "a city of learning" with "no sordid or inharmonious feature."[47]

[43]*Ibid.*

[44]*Harpers Weekly*, October 7, 1899.

[45]Arthur Drexler (ed.), *The Architecture of the École des Beaux Arts* (London, 1977), 40.

[46]Dober, *Campus Planning*, 34.

[47]*Ibid.*, 36.

The significance was seized upon immediately. One English commentator observed that

> the intention is to treat the grounds and buildings together, landscape gardening and architecture forming one composition, which will never need to be structurally changed in all the future history of the university. The architect who can seize the opportunity thus offered will immortalize himself.[48]

Bernard Maybeck's release from teaching duties for two years to travel and explain the Berkeley ideal to likely European competitors was only one part of a sustained effort to show publicly that California was determined to establish its intellectual respectability. Reinstein circulated the presidents of leading universities throughout North America, as well as eminent architects, eliciting ideas on college planning and pressing his vision of a "grand, harmonious scheme which shall contemplate upon this, the noblest site on the earth, the most glorious architectural pile in history."[49] Maybeck traveled to Boston to try to elicit from the American Institute of Architects (AIA) the names of six possible judges for the competition. The AIA was affronted that they were not being asked to organize the whole thing. R. D. Andrews wrote in strong terms to Reinstein in January 1897 explaining the importance of conforming to AIA. practice:

> The immediate cause of my writing to you is the receipt of a request from Mr. Maybeck to write upon a card the names of six architects for judges of the competition for the buildings of the University of California, and to sign the same. I saw Mr. Maybeck in Boston and discussed with him other possible schemes of competition. I have also seen and talked at length with the other men in New York after their interview with Mr. Maybeck. There are so many points of view regarding a matter of this sort that the only dignified, and consequently safe path before you is to appeal to the highest professional board in the country,

---

[48]*The Builder*, 73 (1897): 415.
[49]*California Architect and Building News* (January 1896): 2.

which is the American Institute of Architects, and to ask them for a detailed scheme of competition, or to have them confer with the Regents in regard to the matter in a formal and authorized way. I write this letter and make this suggestion largely because Mr. Maybeck has made this specific demand upon me as noted above. I must refuse to act in this matter as an individual while the important organisation of our profession has not been authoritatively approached.[50]

The editorial policy of the *American Architect and Building News* was to support this line. There was clearly a feeling that Berkeley was seeking to rise above its station and threatening to break with accepted national practice:

A prolonged discussion showed that the committee representing the University had consulted many of the officers of the Institute and its Chapters, as well as other prominent architects, all of whom, it is believed, had advised against an International Competition, and the President of the Institute had already signified that the services of the Institute could be obtained.[51]

The idea of a competition was condemned out of hand by Louis Sullivan, who thought the competition idea to be "wholly fatuous and chimerical, I regard the assumption that you, I or anyone can draw intelligent and just conclusions from a set of sketches . . . to be false, specious and tempting."[52]

Maybeck was left to seek advice elsewhere on the composition of the judging panel. (Figure 10) Garnier became involved shortly before his death and is said to have been keenly interested. It is hardly surprising then that the judges were likely to be predisposed towards a Beaux Arts interpretation of the scheme. J. L. Pascal from France, was himself a Beaux Arts designer and had worked with Bénard for many years. Paul Wallot from Germany was the architect of the new Reichstag building in Berlin. Norman Shaw

[50]*American Architect and Building News*, 55 (March 13, 1897): 87.
[51]*Ibid.*
[52]*California Architect and Building News* 17 (January 1896): 2.

Figure 10: Members of the Competition jury, 1899.

from England was one of the high priests of the currently fashionable Queen Anne revival architecture. Before the second phase of the tournament, he was replaced by John Belcher who had designed the Cambridge Guildhall and authored a book on *The Late-Renaissance in England.* Finally, Walter Cook, the only American judge, had worked in France and Germany and had been for two years president of the Society of Beaux Arts Architects. (It could be argued that the competition was in effect decided before it began!) This all occurred just as the Society of Beaux Arts was circulating its members and advising them only to enter competitions in which the winner would be appointed architect and left to develop the plan in their own way.[53] What Berkeley was suggesting was exactly in line with this demand, and was therefore particularly attractive to Beaux Arts architects.

The local press was in no doubt that the competition marked an opportunity to assert the preeminence of California. The *Berkeley Daily Advocate* anticipated that California's institution would now rise above all others, while the *San Francisco Chronicle* complained that

it is the sneer of Europeans that we call our colleges universities, our seminaries colleges and our schools seminaries; but when the imperial plans for the rehabilitation of our State College have been carried out, Berkeley will stand the peer of Oxford or Cambridge in the ability to interpret and to spread sound learning.[54]

Beyond this, when a dinner was organized for the visiting architects who were taking part in the competition, Phoebe Hearst was so impressed by the potential of the scheme that she observed that a similar competition might be organized for the laying out of the city of San Francisco itself.[55] By December 1898 she had announced a plan for the complete reconstruction of the city of San Francisco, which, as *The Oakland Enquirer* put it,

---

[53]*American Architect and Building News*, 62 (October 8, 1898): 10.

[54]*San Francisco Chronicle* (July 31,1897).

[55]*San Francisco Examiner* (December 4, 1898).

[f]airly takes one's breath away . . . what Mrs. Hearst has in view was somewhat vague, but as near as we can make it out, her idea is that an ideal plan can be drawn for street improvements, including a boulevard system, and a style of construction to be adopted in the erection of business blocks and residences, to which the city may come to conform to some extent in future years.[56]

For his part, emboldened by widening international interest, Jacob Reinstein was able to boast that

[t]his is the first intimation received by the majority of people abroad that the society of the State has emerged from the rough and lawless condition depicted by Bret Harte and writers of his school. . . . The magnificent advertisement that California has received will tend to draw to it a population of high culture.[57]

This determination to assert the cultural preeminence of California was rooted in part in the currently fashionable Anglo-Saxonism that perceived its origins in the literature of Greece and Rome. William R. Davis, president of the Alumni Association, had offered a version of this view in the columns of the *Berkeley Daily Advocate* when the scheme was announced in 1896. "The Anglo-Saxon race is here! New conquests of nature and new advances of man are signified by new walls laid in the Grecian grounds at Berkeley."[58]

Given the natural attraction of the site, it is hardly surprising that enthusiasts for the architectural competition should return repeatedly to the question of how best to realize a "Western Acropolis of Learning."[59] For some, like Professor Despradelle of the Massachusetts Institute of Technology who visited in 1898, this meant planning a campus that would enable the development of athletic prowess:

[56]*Oakland Enquirer* (December 5, 1898).
[57]*San Francisco Chronicle* (November 6, 1898).
[58]*Berkeley Daily Advocate* (October 31, 1896).
[59]*The Investor* (San Francisco), 19, No. 163 (November 1896).

There is nothing like it anywhere in the world. . . . The
grounds are unique and so are all the conditions. . . . . The
only analogy to be drawn is between ancient Greece and
Rome, where they led much the same life of activity and
developed athletic sports along with the intellectual
nature. . . . It must be large, massive, vigorous, radical. The
plan of this competition is such that it ought to bring
classical results.[60]

This view undoubtedly helps to explain the importance for the
planners of the "large drilling and exercizing field . . . for athletic
games" emphasized in the competition brief, which asked that "this
athletic ring should be treated in a monumental and majestic style."
The scheme also insisted on a drill field for exercises in the open
air, since "all the able-bodied male students receive military
instruction twice a week."[61] The *American Architect and Building
News* made a great play of this emphasis on the military, commenting that there was demanded

an open-air drill field, sheltered courts for drilling twelve
companies of infantry, one company of engineers, a
squadron of cavalry and a battery of artillery, an armory, an
auditorium for 5000 people . . . and all planned with the
assumption that there will ultimately be 5000 students. . . .
No precedent has been found at other universities to
determine the space required to provide for the military
establishment proposed at Berkeley. Cornell provides one
and a half acres for an armory and parade ground, and at the
University of Minnesota the armory covers one half acre
and an adjacent athletic field two acres. A competent
authority states that a drill field for exercises in the open air
should be not less than two acres in extent.[62]

This aspect of the competition was seized upon by Emile
Bénard for his winning submission: it was the plans of the univer-

[60]*San Francisco Chronicle* (November 27, 1898).
[61]*Program for an International Competition for the Phoebe Hearst
Architectural Plan for the University of California* (Berkeley, 1897), 20-21.
[62]*American Architect and Building News*, 61 (July 16, 1898): 20-22.

Figure 11: Emile Bénard, winner of first prize, "Perspective View of Stadium."

sity gymnasia that he chose to submit in detail. (Figure 11) For others, though, the importance of this classical tradition was simply that students should be brought, through their environment, to a respect for the ancient world and its values. Professor Charles Elliot Norton of Harvard summarized this view in his enthusiastic response to Reinstein's enquiry:

> For it is these arts, properly called the humanities, which set the standard of human attainment. . . . The youth who lives surrounded by beautiful and dignified buildings . . . cannot but be strongly affected . . . by the constant presence of objects that cultivate his sense of beauty, and arouse his sympathy with the spirit and generous efforts of his distant predecessors.[63]

Reinstein himself was an unabashed enthusiast for the project they were undertaking:

> let us build slowly yet grandly that there may greet the commerce which shall whiten the Golden gate and the civilisation which shall grace this Western shore an architectural pile of stately and glorious buildings, which shall rival the dreams of the builders of the Columbian exposition, which shall do honour and justice to a superb Republic, . . . and which shall, even in their ruins, strike the beholder with wonder and rapture.[64]

When the preliminary results were announced, all 11 premiated architects were graduates of the École des Beaux Arts. (Figure 12) This was to prove the most controversial aspect of the competition. One leading British journal, *The Builder*, saw this as a wilful favoring of things French,

> unless French training really is superior to any other in enabling architects to deal with large schemes of design. . . . The shape of the French Renaissance in conceptions of the whole scheme suggests the Paris Exhibition rather than a university. . . . There must be other bases of design than French Renaissance which could be made

---

[63]*Berkeley Daily Advocate* (May 2, 1896).
[64]*California Architect and Building News* (January 1896): 2.

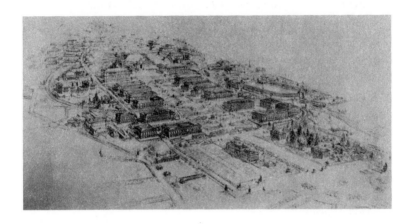

Figure 12: Emile Bénard, first prize, "General Perspective."

effective in a monumental group of university buildings. . . . Many of the most important monuments in the
world are Gothic. . . . These graduates of the École des
Beaux Arts seem to believe that architecture means French
Renaissance, whatever purpose is to be served.[65]

Similarly, Norman Shaw, the English judge for the first phase of the
competition, expressed his regret that none of the English entries
had been selected, although he accepted that the cleverness of the
French-influenced designs distinguished them from the others
submitted. He conceded the excellence of this French school, and
admitted that "architecture is more thoroughly taught in France than
in England . . . and this no doubt, accounts for its character being
stamped on all chosen plans. It must also be remembered that
English architects have always been weak in public buildings, but
excel in private houses, churches, etc., while the French are the
reverse."[66] But it is important to remember that what was being
attempted at Berkeley was a variant of the French Beaux Arts style
that enabled the campus to announce itself as being at once
Californian and yet within the broad European tradition. Locally,
E. B. Payne summarized this in the *Overland Monthly* in 1899,
pointing out that although Bénard was a copyist, he captured

the genius and spirit of that entire southern development of
architecture. . . . We have before us in California a Classic
conception, allying us, through France and Italy, with the
early and superlative genius that wrought beside the
Aegean sea. But . . . we produce results bearing true and
characteristic marks of our own, our thought and purpose
and meanings. . . . What is essential to our humanity in
California ought to be built into the walls of our City of
Education.[67]

The editorial tone of the *California Architect* was more
ambivalent, unsure that it was appropriate to draw so heavily upon
a single architectural tradition:

[65]*The Builder*, 77 (1899): 524.
[66]University Archives, Hearst competition press notices (308 gh pr. vi).
[67]*Overland Monthly* (November 1899): 446-55.

[a]s to the style of the selected plans it is known that, generally, they are of the French school, certainly the most admirable in the world, a school that has supplied California with some of its most eminent architects, yet to many it would be disappointing to learn that the Regents of the University of California should adopt any school so distinctly national as the French as the style in which these buildings are to be erected. In the opinion of some thoughtful men, there are signs of the development of a new school of architecture, composite it may be, but sufficiently distinctive of our own clime and appropriate to our national life. So splendid an example of college architecture as the university buildings are expected to be will afford an opportunity for the introduction of new ideas embodying in it the traditions, hopes and ambitions of the most lavishly endowed state.[68]

Similarly, G. Héraud, one of the French entrants in the competition, argued in the *San Francisco Examiner* for something more distinctively native:

As to the style of architecture for it, I think it should not be Grecian, or Italian, or to represent any foreign country or past age, but perhaps to partake a little of all, and over and above all to typify, in its interpretation, America and Americans.

I noticed in New York buildings of the Louis XVI style of architecture and of the Florentine and other eras, but in my opinion these are unsuited to the proposed great university, and to the buildings generally of this country. What it wants is something characteristic of itself, with perhaps touches of the styles of the old world.[69]

E. B. Payne, a well-known local figure, was more scathing in his comments:

We can hardly expect to have a distinct national architecture here in the United States . . . a reign of caprice and

---

[68]University Archives, Hearst Competition press notices.
[69]*San Francisco Examiner* (December 13, 1898).

general eclecticism held sway even among the better architects; for being suddenly brought face to face through travel and literature with so many foreign styles, it was as though a tribe of savages had discovered a theatrical wardrobe, and each masqueraded in the manner which pleased him best.[70]

In the event, Bénard's winning design packed more buildings onto the site than any other entrant, all focused on the central avenue running down towards the Golden Gate. Another echo of Olmsted's original plan was the continuation of the main avenue by a tree-lined lawn running on up the hill. The lower cross axis of Bénard's design allowed for humanities buildings to be arranged symmetrically around the library square, a second cross axis generated a science square, all planned in such a way that future expansion was possible without destroying the overall scheme.

Once the result was known the American architectural press became more ready to sympathize with the Berkeley regents, commenting that what really mattered was not the question of whether or not the campus was built on the lines of the winning entry, so much as the fact that a major international architectural competition had been carried through successfully.[71]

No sooner was Bénard identified as the winner early in 1900, than difficulties began to pile in. He was personally difficult, and spoke little English. He appeared unwilling to stay and commit himself to the development of the plan. By the beginning of 1901 these difficulties were coming to a head. Before the end of January President Benjamin Ide Wheeler and Phoebe Hearst were discussing in their correspondence who would be best to replace him. Maybeck wanted Despradelle, who had entered the original competition, but Wheeler persuaded him that John Galen Howard should be their choice:

He agreed with me that probably Mr. Howard represented the line of least resistance when all the difficulties were

---

[70]*Overland Monthly* (November 1899): 446-55.
[71]*American Architect and Building News*, 65 (September 23,1899): 97.

considered. I think Mr. Maybeck while preferring Mr. Despradelle, thinks Mr. Howard the next best man and recognizes that he is a delightful personality. . . . Mr Maybeck is particularly anxious to have a Frenchman occupy the position: he says it would smooth things over with the people in Paris. I myself do not think this is necessary. Mr. Bénard has received ample remuneration and glory for all he has done. . . . If Mr. Howard is the right man, why should we not go ahead?[72]

Within a few days Phoebe Hearst had sent on a telegram to Bénard dispensing with his services, a communication that elicited a sharp response from the French architect, asking on what grounds the decision had been made.[73] (Figures 13 and 14) But, as John Galen Howard was drawn in during the following months to turn the scheme into a reality, the dissatisfactions with Bénard's work mounted. In mid-March 1901 Howard and Wheeler walked the grounds together: Howard pointed out that the central axis of the campus had been located by Bénard in the wrong place, causing enormous unnecessary excavation; his elevations for the Mining Building (which Phoebe Hearst saw as the jewel in the crown) were three feet out at the North East Corner. Wheeler's report of all this to Mrs. Hearst shows his growing sense of exasperation:

I cannot understand what M. Bénard could have been thinking of. It seems hardly possible that he could have even looked at the ground. . . . You need not worry about all this. Mr. Howard will adjust the whole plan to reasonableness. I only wrote to you about it in order that you may appreciate how ludicrous much of the original plan was. Mr. Howard thinks that the main features of the plan are excellent and can be used.[74]

A week later, Wheeler's criticisms were even more pungent:

The more I study the plan of M. Bénard and the more that I become acquainted with all that it involves, the more

---

[72]University Archives, Presidents' records, CU 5/ 7:168.
[73]*Ibid.*
[74]*Ibid.*

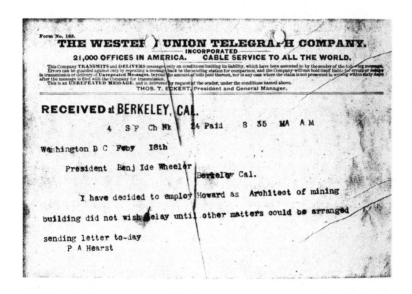

Figure 13: (top) Secret message to Phoebe Hearst suggesting a change of architect, February 15, 1901. Figure 14: (bottom) Telegram to President Wheeler from Mrs. Hearst with decision to employ John Galen Howard, February 18, 1901.

certain I am that he dealt with his work rather as a problem for creating a picture on paper than for locating buildings on the earth. . . . I do not think it right that we should undertake a plan which would involve five to ten million dollars of expenditure for grading. . . . M. Bénard is aware that his plan has not progressed sufficiently to be workable. . . . The most serious oversight in it seems to be this: the main axis of the plan steers for University Avenue instead of for the Golden Gate. . . . If this axis were used the amount of grading would be reduced to a minimum. M. Bénard's plan arranges the grounds according to the streets of the present Berkeley instead of according to the great features of the landscape. . . . M. Bénard has been fully remunerated for the work which he has done and his work has come to a definite conclusion. It is understood by Mr. Howard and everybody that M. Bénard's plans are to be the basis for the work which is to be undertaken from this time on.[75]

By the beginning of April 1901, Phoebe Hearst was confirming her agreement that the main axis of the plan should be in line with the Golden Gate, adding bitterly her observation that "I have felt all the time that it was Bénard's intention to confuse the plan so that he would have to be employed to work it out."[76]

So, almost by accident, the Berkeley regents drew back from Bénard's monumental and heavily decorated version of the French Beaux Arts style, and from the details of campus layout that he had proposed. It was a circumstance that gave enormous authority to his successor, John Galen Howard, to reinterpret the scheme as he saw fit. (Figure 15)

By the end of 1901, Howard, who, as we have seen, was well-versed in all aspects of recent Californian development, had been given the contract for the Mining Building, which was to become one of the enduring glories of the campus. So, Howard became the superintending architect, a nd in 1903, head of the newly created

---

[75]*Ibid.*
[76]*Ibid.*

Roy Lowe

Figure 15: John Galen Howard's plan for the Berkeley campus, 1917.

Department of Architecture, a post that he held until his retirement in 1927. Thus, almost by accident, John Galen Howard, who was a forceful and dedicated man, became the presiding genius: much of what we see today was his doing, the Doe Library, California Hall, Durant Hall, Hilgard Hall, Wheeler Hall, Sather Gate, and the campanile were all designed by him. He was acceptable partly because of his commitment to a gradual development of the site that would reflect the organic growth of both the university and the state, and that was four square within the principles of Beaux Arts planning. As one commentator put it:

> [i]t may require twenty-five or even fifty years. . . . Thus, it will arise in this new modern time, and on this advanced shore of the world's progress, somewhat as the grand cathedrals of Europe arose . . . its course laid in that fidelity which affirms and reaffirms a noble purpose, its completion ensured in the constancy of a people enamoured of a sacred idea.[77]

This agreed precisely with the vision of President Wheeler, who wrote in 1899 that

> The university stands by the gates of that sea upon which the Twentieth century is to see the supreme conflict between the two great world halves. It is set to be the intellectual representative of the front rank of occidentalism, the rank that will lead the change or bear the shock. In the Old World struggle between the east and west, the Aegean was the arena and occidentalism militant faced east, orientalism west; in the new struggles occidentalism faces west, orientalism east. The arena is the Pacific.[78]

A recent historian summarizes the outcome in a similar fashion. "The Pacific was the new Aegean, Berkeley was the new Athens, the University, the new Acropolis. In Howard's plan the vocabulary of the ancient classical world and the dynamic and idealistic spirit

---

[77]*Overland Monthly* (October 1899): 353-61.

[78]Benjamin Ide Wheeler in *Land of Sunshine*, 12 (1899), 4, quoted by Partridge, *Howard*, 21.

of his Beaux-Arts classical style were to animate the City of Learning."[79]

The determination to devise a city of learning that would mark California's emergence from barbarity coincided with the emergence of a Californian style and also with American susceptibility to the City Beautiful movement, which drew from European traditions of town planning. Throw in the tensions that existed between northern and southern models of university architecture, and the ingredients were present for an architectural achievement that was unique. Stanford offered one model of a mission style architecture that clearly stated California's special Mediterranean heritage and its "El Dorado" self-conception. At one level this version of Romanesque might have been appropriate for Berkeley. But Anglo-Saxonism demanded a statement, how clear is perhaps not the issue, that the state university was four square within a northern European tradition. English versions of collegiate Gothic never came under serious consideration, perhaps because they suggested a cloistered, inward looking community and an academic tradition that was at variance with these Californian aspirations for a city of learning that would in all senses constitute a state within the state.

Phoebe Hearst was a lifelong Francophile. Hausmann's achievements in Paris had only underlined the ability of French architects to cope with town planning in a monumental manner; the dazzle of the City Beautiful movement for North Americans was brought into focus at the Chicago World's Fair. All the preconditions were present for an attempt to define the unique potentialities of California in its university through a Beaux Arts campus. At a moment, when around the English speaking world, universities were seeking to lay claim to preeminence through their architecture, the precise mode in which the regents of the university of California chose to articulate their aspirations was one that could not have been hit upon anywhere else. In this sense, the Berkeley campus is unique.

---

[79]*Ibid.*